LAYERS OF LIFE

A leafcutter ant uses its scissorlike mandibles to cut out a section of leaf. Once the fragment is removed, this ant will join a column of thousands, each bringing their own piece of leaf back to the nest.

Deep in the Amazon

LAYERS OF LIFE

by James L. Castner

BENCHMARK BOOKS

MARSHALL CAVENDISH
NEW YORK

With thanks to Dr. Gary Hartshorn, Organization for Tropical Studies, Duke University, for his careful review of the manuscript.

Benchmark Books
Marshall Cavendish Corporation
99 White Plains Road
Tarrytown, New York 10591-9001
www.marshallcavendish.com

• • •

Library of Congress Cataloging-in-Publication Data
Castner, James L.
Layers of Life / by James L. Castner
p. cm—(Deep in the Amazon)
Includes bibliographical references (p.) and index
ISBN 0-7614-1130-5
1. Rain forest ecology—Amazon River Watershed—Juvenile literature.
[1. Rain forest ecology—Amazon River Region. 2. Ecology. 3. Amazon River Region.] I. Title.
QH112 .C36 2001   577.34'0981'1—dc21   2001 025472

• • •

Printed in Hong Kong
1 3 5 7 8 6 4 2

• • •

Book Designer: Judith Turziano
Photo Research: Candlepants Incorporated

• • •

CREDITS
Cover Photo: Corbis / Tom Brakefield
The photographs in this book are used by permission and through the courtesy of:
Photo Researchers: Gary Retherford, title page. *Corbis*: Owen Frank, 8;
Michael & Patricia Fogden, 11,12, 32, 49, 50(bottom), 52, 58; Wolfgang Kaehler, 14, 17, 22,
24, 38; Jim Zuckerman, 16; Brian Vikander, 18; Alison Wright, 33; Kevin Schafer, 34,
43, 45; Kennan Ward, 36; Steve Chenn, 37; Tom Brakefield, 42. *James L. Castner:* 20, 25,
26, 27, 28, 30, 41, 44, 46, 48, 50(top), 57. *Peter Arnold*: Still Pictures, 54.

CONTENTS

VENEZUELA

Orinoco

COLOMBIA

Branco

Napo River

Rio Negro

Amazon River

Macapá

Equator

ECUADOR

Iquitos

Manaus

Belém

Amazon River Basin

PERU

BRAZIL

Lake Titicaca

BOLIVIA

ANDES MOUNTAINS

Amazon River Basin

○ Author's field sites

Average annual rainfall:
50–175 inches (130–445 centimeters)

Average temperature:
80° Fahrenheit (27° Celsius)

0   600 miles

0   900 kilometers

AUTHOR'S NOTE

In the tropical rain forest, the thick foliage and wild growth seem to close in around you. The forest floor is often clearly visible only when you are standing on a trail. It is easy to notice only those things directly in front of you. Biologists who study the creatures of the rain forest are often guilty of exploring those areas just within their reach. Bird-watchers, on the other hand, gaze up into the trees, completely ignoring the forest floor.

There are many parts to the rain forest. They include not only the lower forest, but the canopy and other layers that tower high above it. Recent advances have made it possible to reach those upper levels. Scientists have found new ways to climb the trees more easily. They have also built walkways and observation platforms up in the treetops. They can now study and collect organisms from all levels of this complex ecosystem. From the leaf-covered ground to the tallest emergent trees, let's explore these layers and observe some of the rain forest's fascinating creatures.

As the forest often grows as one continuous mass, it is hard to see its layers and many parts. Paddling one of the region's many waterways sometimes offers a better view.

Chapter One

DIVIDING THE FOREST

When you look up from the forest floor, it is hard to imagine that this lush world can be divided into layers. It looks instead like one ongoing ceiling of green. Branches of small trees and countless palms tend to hide the crowns, or tops, of the trees that make up the upper forest. But if we could take a slice, a cross-section of the rain forest, a new impression would emerge. Then we could see that the Amazon forest is actually made up of several living layers, each with its own unique plants and animals.

These layers do not always divide at exactly the same place. Instead, one level often blends into the next without a clear sense of beginning or end. Not all scientists define the same number of layers, but most tropical biologists agree that there are four. The two layers that are easiest to isolate are those at the extremes—the forest floor and the emergents, or tallest trees. They are at opposite ends of the dense and often tangled layers that occur in between.

The forest floor is easy to find. We're standing on it. It is a thin layer of soil covered with leaf litter, broken branches, and pieces of bark and plants that have fallen from above. Moving up, we enter the understory. It is made up of bushes, shrubs, vines, and small trees. Above that, the canopy forms the roof of the rain forest. It is the canopy you can see from the air. The trees generally grow together, making the rain forest appear to be an endless "sea of green." Finally come the rainforest giants that spread their crowns even higher than the canopy. The emergents sometimes tower as much as 250 feet (76 meters) above the forest floor. They are at the fringe of the other layers that together form the forest. The layers are all parts of a whole. Through examining each of them, it is easier to gain a better understanding of a tropical forest.

Whether flying above, boating alongside, or walking within the tropical forest, one sees trees everywhere. Crowns and branches, trunks and leaves, trees give the forest its shape. The trees and plants of the rain forest serve many functions. They are crucial to its many living residents. They provide food and shelter to a wealth of species. The animals rely on the trees as much as the trees rely on the animals. It is a partnership that targets survival.

The Food Factor

A caterpillar munches on a leaf. The leftovers are carried away by a leafcutter ant. The millions of plant-eating insect species that live in the Amazon Basin rely on trees as a food source. They are found in the entire length of the forest—from immature cicadas attached to the roots all the way up to tiny fly larvae called leaf miners. They feed on the tissue between layers of canopy leaves.

From time to time, giant tropical trees burst into flower. Often, when flying low over the rain forest I have seen splashes of vibrant yellow and swaths of pink. These bright colors mark the places where entire trees have broken into bloom. Flowers provide a feast for bees, wasps, and butterflies. But the sugary nectar most flowers produce to attract these pollinators draws other rainforest creatures as well. Birds, small mammals, and sometimes bats are also frequent visitors. These creatures feed on the nectar as well. In doing so, they transfer pollen from flower to flower and from tree to tree. This process, called pollination, allows the trees to reproduce and to create fruits and seeds.

The fruits that trees produce are another valuable food source. Many

A coatimundi balances atop a bunch of bananas. Fruit lovers, coatis are scavengers with a wide-ranging appetite. They search the trees as well as the ground for seeds, eggs, and a variety of small organisms including insects and mice.

species of fig trees grow throughout the forest and provide a bounty for birds and mammals. Frugivorous, or fruit-eating, species of bats search at night to locate a ripe, dangling fruit for their meal. Monkeys and coatimundis feast on fruits in the trees. But their antics often cause ripe fruits to fall to the ground. A certain portion will wind up on the forest floor anyway, as animals seldom find every one. These fallen fruits, half squashed and often broken open from the impact, now become potential food for all the ground-dwelling animals as well. Rodents, armadillos, opossums, peccaries, and even large, cowlike tapirs may sample this fallen food. Even a fallen piece of fruit, knocked off by a hasty monkey, shows the living connection between the forest's many creatures. Without intending to, the monkey is assisting the organisms that forage on the forest floor.

Tree House

Trees also serve as the homes or shelters for countless Amazonian animals. In the case of insects, they may bore in the wood, hollow out a twig, camouflage themselves along the bark, or even weave together several leaves. Birds are another common resident of the trees. Hummingbirds create tiny cup-sized nests lined with lichens. Some are built low enough

Trees provide homes and roosts that keep some animals hidden from predators and out of harm's way. Here a group of tent-making bats clusters together beneath a heliconia leaf. By carefully cutting the leaf, these clever engineers form a little tent in which they can safely nestle.

to be seen from the ground. Oropendolas, on the other hand, weave dangling nests, 5 to 6 feet (1.5–1.8 m) long, in the treetops. Woodpeckers drill their own homes. Later when they are abandoned, the openings provide ready-made shelters for rodents and small mammals. This is yet another example of one species indirectly helping another.

The forest is full of potential homes. The top of an old hollow tree may serve as a roost for bats, while various mammals at ground level could find shelter at the bottom. Snakes, lizards, frogs, and tarantulas also make excellent use of the nooks and crannies of hollow limbs they find on trees. They even use the epiphytes as well. These are plants that grow directly on trees, often high in the air.

It would be almost impossible to look closely at any part of a rainforest tree and not find an organism living there. Plus the rain forest offers such a diverse range of choices. Trees differ in their size and shape, the width of their trunks, the texture of their bark, the length and thickness of their leaves, and in the protective chemicals they contain. Many animals have evolved in direct response to these different offerings. Their bodies have adapted, or changed, so that they are better suited for living in a small portion of the environment. As animals become more specialized, or adapted, they compete less with one another for space. This is one of the reasons the rain forests of the Amazon can house the millions of species it does. If animals share the trees by living in different parts of them, a specific tree or a whole tract of forest can support a more diverse range of life.

Leaves are the sites of some of the rain forest's most fascinating, yet hidden, processes. They are mini factories and distribution centers. They make their own food and transport water and nutrients.

Chapter Two

CYCLES OF LIFE

*T*he life-forms found in the tropical forests of the Amazon Basin are more diverse than any other place on Earth. Their success depends on how well they interact with one another. But it is also linked to the nonliving portions of the environment over which they have no control. These nonliving, or abiotic, elements include rainfall, soil, light, heat, wind, and nutrients. They are being constantly used, shared, cycled, or recycled to the benefit of each plant and animal. Just as important, though, is the role they play in helping the rain forest to thrive and sustain itself. The water cycle and the nutrient cycle are two of these life-giving processes.

The Water Cycle

If you look at a map of Peru showing the country's climate zones, you may be in for a few surprises. While the eastern slopes of the Andes are covered with lush forests and tropical foliage, the western, or Pacific, slopes of the mountain chain are dry. They lead down to coastal deserts. These deserts found along the coasts of Peru and Chile are some of the most arid places in the world. In fact, some areas have never recorded any rainfall. So why is there such a difference from one side of the Andes to the other? The answer has to do with air currents and the process by which moisture makes its way to the ground.

In the regions near the equator, the sun beats down on the land a pre-

The eastern slopes of the Andes are home to lush mountain forests that are continually cloaked in clouds. As these clouds rise and cool, they release their moisture.

dictable twelve hours a day. This solar energy heats the air and causes it to rise. The air carries with it water vapor, which collects in the form of clouds. The Andes Mountains form a barrier to these clouds and their moisture-rich air. They force them to rise higher in order to move through. As the air rises, it cools and the clouds release the moisture they contain. This precipitation takes the form of rain at lower altitudes and snow at higher elevations. By the time the air makes it over the Andes to reach the coast, practically all of its moisture is gone. This process is known as the rain shadow effect. Rain falls on one side of the mountains before the clouds can pass over them.

An enormous amount of water flows from the Amazon's mouth into the Atlantic Ocean each day. Some of this water comes back as precipitation, carried by trade winds that blow west across the Atlantic. The vast forest itself and the bodies of water found within it are other sources of precipitation. Water evaporates into the atmosphere and also hitches a ride on these winds. Much of the rain and snow that fall on the eastern side of the Andes is added to the headwaters of the Amazon and the other rivers of the

Upper Amazon. The headwaters is the place where a river begins.

The movement of water from air to forest and back to the air again is known as the water cycle. To start the cycle, rain falls on the Amazon Basin. About one-fourth of this moisture returns to the air through evaporation from lakes and rivers. Another fourth evaporates directly from the surfaces of the leaves without ever reaching the ground. The remaining half of the water is returned through the trees themselves. These are, of course, estimates. The rainfall that makes it to the ground and seeps into the soil is picked up by roots and taken into the transport system of the tree. It flows up through tubes within the stem or trunk until it reaches the leaves.

All plants with green leaves use light and the sun's energy to fuel photosynthesis. Through this process, the plant or tree creates its own sugary

Water, water, everywhere. The rivers of the Amazon Basin, such as this one in eastern Ecuador, are the most obvious source. Yet a lot of water is also contained in the forest's plants and trees. It is drawn up by the roots and eventually released through the leaves.

form of food. Carbon dioxide and all-important water are turned into sugar molecules and oxygen. The carbon dioxide is taken from the atmosphere. It is the basis for the chemical reactions that occur within the leaf. If the surface of the leaf is kept moist, the carbon dioxide needed for photosynthesis can dissolve and be drawn inside. However, much of the water that has passed through the plant evaporates from the leaf's surface. But through the ongoing water cycle, more moisture is on its way. It is an ingredient necessary to survival.

The Nutrient Cycle

The tropical soils of the Amazon are very different from those found in temperate forests. If we examined the soil found in a forest in the United States, we would see a layer of leaf litter on the surface that may be 10 to 12 inches (25.4–30.5 cm) deep. Beneath this is a thick layer of nutrient-rich topsoil. Altogether, this fertile upper layer of topsoil may reach more than 6 feet (1.8 m). As a result, the roots of temperate trees tend to grow deep.

The thin leaf litter and shallow topsoil of a tropical forest support an amazing diversity of trees, shrubs, and plants. Some, such as this vine, use nearby trees for support.

Nutrients are found scattered throughout the entire layer.

The ground beneath an Amazonian forest shows a completely different structure and distribution of nutrients. If we looked beneath a forest in Peru or Ecuador, we would immediately notice a thin layer of leaf litter. It might even be less than 1 inch (2.5 cm) deep. This is largely due to the tropical environment. In the Amazon Basin, fallen leaves and other debris from the forest do not have a chance to build up. These materials quickly decompose, broken down by the hot, humid climate of the rain forest. The climate of a rain forest is ideally suited to rapidly decompose once-living matter. Whether a fallen leaf, a dead bird, or animal droppings, the high heat, humidity, and rainfall combine to make short work of them. Once these dead or excreted items have been broken down, the nutrients they contained become available. They are quickly absorbed and used by the surrounding plants and trees. Most of these essential nutrients are stored within the leaves, branches, bark, trunks, and roots of the living forest.

The topsoil beneath the leaf litter is often no more than 2 to 4 inches (5 to 10 cm) deep. This offers only a very shallow layer for trees to use. Tropical trees have adapted to take the best advantage of this limited amount of nutrients. They tend to develop a wide, shallow network of roots. Often the roots grow in an almost horizontal fashion parallel to the ground. Trees and plants, like any other organism in the rain forest, need certain essential nutrients if they are to grow, thrive, and reproduce. But if the nutrients are so necessary, why are such limited amounts found in tropical soils? They are quickly snatched up and used by the forest's many other trees.

A tropical forest is a living storehouse of nutrients. They spend only a brief part of the entire cycle in the soil itself. Most of the time nutrients form parts of the molecules that make up plants and animals. Thus the nutrient cycle is a waiting game. The death of one organism frees its nutrients and thus aids the life of another. As with water, it is this cycling and sharing that help keep the rain forest and its many residents alive.

In the cycling of nutrients, fungi play a major role. They are eaten by the larvae of fungus beetles such as this one.

Chapter Three

LIFE AMONG THE LITTER

*T*he layer of leaf litter covering the forest floor tends to be thin. But that doesn't mean it isn't teeming with life. Down among the clutter and debris, often too small for the eyes to see, live some of the rain forest's tiniest residents. They are small creatures with a big job to do. For it is here that the important task of decomposition is constantly carried out. If it weren't for this breakdown of once-living material, the vines and plants, the tall trees towering above—the entire forest—would starve for lack of nutrients. But due to the climate of the rain forest and these hardworking decomposers, the breakdown of matter can be a rapid process. Nutrients are swiftly recycled and returned to the living creatures that rely on them.

When a leaf floats down from the canopy to the forest floor, there is a host of organisms waiting to attack it. The same holds true if it were an entire tree crashing to the ground. The combined efforts of bacteria, fungi, and invertebrates such as termites may reduce the leaf to its basic elements in a few weeks. Naturally a full-grown tree takes longer, often several years. Nonetheless, it is part of an essential process that shows how connected the forest's layers truly are. The green leaves of the tallest emergents depend on the nutrients processed by the often microscopic organisms living far below.

Fungi are perhaps the most unappreciated organisms in the rain forest. Like all decomposers, they are classified as saprophytes. This means they

A few unusual species of fungi are parasitic and actually attack insects. Here a beetle has been killed by a parasitic fungus, which has grown long stalks from its body.

get their nutrients from breaking down organic material, or matter that was once alive. Perhaps the best-known part of a fungus is the reproductive structure that bears the spores. This is called a mushroom. However, the main body of a fungus, the hypha, is hidden within the litter or soil. When many hyphae grow together in a network of thin strands they are called a mycelium. They are like tiny threadlike roots that often extend throughout the leaf litter and directly into rotting logs and branches. Carefully sifting through the forest litter, leaf by leaf, will often reveal the hyphae. At times they may even be visible on the surface.

Mushrooms come in many shapes and colors. I have picked up rotting twigs adorned with transparent mushrooms that looked like fine crystal glassware. At other times, I have observed tiny cup fungi clustered on a fallen log. Their red pigment contrasts sharply with the background of brown bark. Large bracket fungi abound in the rain forest as well. They turn up wherever there is rotting wood. These fungi are often infested with the larvae of fungus-feeding beetles.

Perhaps the most spectacular of mushrooms is the veiled lady. This unusual fungus seldom lasts for more than a day. It belongs to the group known as stinkhorns. It is an appropriate name for it gives off an extremely unpleasant odor that is used to attract flies that help scatter its spores. Standing 4 to 5 inches (10–12.5 cm) high, it sports a white, netlike veil that reaches from its rounded brown top to the ground. This species is impossible to mistake either by its appearance or its smell.

There is another group of fungi called the mycorrhizae that is of great importance to many rainforest trees. The mycorrhizal fungi live in close association with the roots. Sometimes they even invade the root tissue. They serve as a type of bridge, sending important nutrients directly to the tree's rootlets where they will be absorbed. Thus, not only do they break down the debris and organic matter, they also personally deliver the nutrients to the roots. Otherwise the tree would have to remove the nutrients from the soil itself. Substances such as nitrogen, phosphorus, potassium, and zinc become available to the tree much more quickly when presented by the mycorrhizal fungi. They have evolved more efficient methods for removing them from the soil. In return for their help, the

Mushrooms such as these delicate cup fungi adorn the forest floor. Diversity, or the range of species present, is just as high in the world of fungi as it is with other rainforest organisms.

fungi are provided with sugars, which the tree produces as a result of photosynthesis. This type of partnership, in which both organisms benefit, is known as mutualism.

Another special partnership exists between trees and plants called legumes and some types of bacteria found in the soil. Legumes are in the bean and pea family. They produce fruit in the form of a flat pod. The bacteria are called nitrogen-fixing bacteria. They have the valuable talent of being able to take nitrogen from the air and package it into a solid form called ammonium nitrate. This can then be used by the plants. On their own, legumes cannot use the nitrogen as it exists in the air. So, many legume trees have developed rounded nodules at their roots. This is where the bacteria live. Just as with the mycorrhizal fungi, in this case of mutualism the bacteria receive sugars from the tree. At the same time, they are given a protected living space within the nodules of the root.

Not all of the decomposers on the forest floor are microscopic. There are a wealth of creatures known as macroinvertebrates, which are large animals without backbones. In most cases they are insects and their rela-

Many scavengers that live on the rainforest floor are dull colored. This cloud forest millipede is unusual with its bright colors, a sure sign that it is foul tasting or maybe even poisonous.

tives. These include scavengers that feed on rotting plant or animal material, like the slow-moving millipedes. With their flattened, armored shell, they look like mechanical toys moving among the leaves. Termites are also important to most tropical rain forests. They are one of the few creatures able to eat and digest wood and dried leaf matter. Actually, the woody material is broken down by one-celled organisms called protozoans, which live within the termite's digestive system. In some areas termites may process as much as 5 percent of the leaf litter. The nests of these social insects are often above ground and easy to spot—just look for a brown bulge on the side of a tree. Dark lines that are actually small covered tunnels lead away from the main nest and down the trunk of the tree. Although small creatures, their total numbers in Amazonian forests are quite large. Not only does their feeding make the litter easy to process for fungi and bacteria, but their abandoned nests add large amounts of nutrients to the soil. This increases its fertility.

Other ground insects focus their efforts on two extremely important

Although many termite nests are no bigger than your fist, some are as large as a basketball. Some even reach the size of the wheel of a car. All hold thousands of termites that feed on cellulose, the woody material in trees and plants.

A large horned dung beetle searches for animal waste that it will roll into a ball. Once away from the main dung pile, the female beetle will lay her egg in the ball. Then together the dung beetles will bury it.

resources—dung and carrion. Dung in the form of animal droppings draws various insects, but mostly the dung beetles. Often large, they are creatures that mold a portion of the droppings into a ball. A male and female will roll the dung ball a safe distance from the other dung beetles. They bury it with an egg inside. The egg then hatches into a larva that feeds on the nutrients in the dung until it develops into an adult.

When animals die or are killed by a predator, the carcass or body is called carrion. Flies that specialize in carrion are often able to detect it minutes after an animal has died. Both flies and certain beetles will feed on the carcass. They can reduce the remains of even a large mammal to little more than a skeleton in less than a week.

Walking through the rain forest through the scatter of debris and dead leaves, it is hard to picture all this activity taking place beneath your feet. Yet fungi, bacteria, and insects are constantly breaking down organic materials. They are workers and providers. They funnel nutrients directly into the trees. Or they free them into the soil where the tangled root systems draw them up. The tallest trees need these tiny assistants. The health and success of the rain forest depend on them.

Wide, flat buttress roots are visible on the trunks of many rainforest trees. They are an adaptation that gives the tree stability. Here, the 6-foot-tall (1.8-m) author is dwarfed by the huge buttresses of a ceiba, or silk cotton, tree.

Chapter Four

THE UNDERSTORY

*T*here is a part of the forest where plants live in semidarkness. They make the most of the scant sunlight that filters down from the canopy. This is the understory, where plants and trees generally grow no higher than 30 to 40 feet (9–12 m). It is a world of ferns and mosses and herbaceous plants scattered among the trunks of rainforest giants. Small shade-tolerant species of trees poke their way through the growth. Some of the things living here will look very familiar to us. Others will appear a bit more bizarre. Either way, all of the understory's residents have learned to cope with low light, low wind, and the rain forest's high humidity.

When I first started working in Amazonian forests, I was surprised at the ease with which I could make my way through the trees. Of course there were spots where the vegetation was thick, but nothing like the dense wall of green I had expected. There was no need to hack a path with a machete. My notion of the rain forest was based on views of the forest's edge. There, abundant light results in a tangled mat of shrubs, creepers, and climbing vines. The dimly lit interior of the forest does not allow such wild growth. Only when a fallen tree opens a gap in the canopy do we see a sudden burst of life. Direct sunlight streams in and coaxes seedlings to break through the soil. But over time the gap fills in and shade returns—the typical conditions of the understory.

The understory plants and trees have undergone many adaptations. One

The strange flowers of the swamp cacao found on the trunk provide an example of cauliflory. Only a short distance above the ground, there they can be seen more easily by understory pollinators.

of the most important is the ability to grow without receiving direct sunlight. But there are other adjustments some trees have made that allow them to thrive beneath the sun-blocking giants high above. The stilt palm is a common yet hearty understory tree. It is easy to identify at ground level due to the cluster of spiny stiltlike roots at its base. At times these slender palms are knocked over and crushed by larger canopy trees when they fall. But if the trunk is not broken, this palm is able to survive even while lying on the ground. In fact, it will send out additional stilt roots farther up the trunk. These allow the tree to once again grow vertically. The result is a crooked tree with a sharply angled trunk.

Another understory adaptation is cauliflory, or flowers and fruit that appear on the tree trunk rather than at the tips of the branches in the crown. Flowers growing on the trunk in low light are often more visible to the animals that aid pollination. Forest floor animals can also access the large fruits that grow on some species that display cauliflory. In this way, the tree recruits additional seed dispersers. It is a role the animals could not play if the fruits were not so close to the ground.

Equally surprising to me was the number of "house plants" I saw all around. Species such as dumbcane, prayer plant, white sails, and parlor ivy add to the understory's diverse life. Plants that my mother had difficulty keeping alive back in New Jersey obviously thrived here in their native habitat. In fact, even the worst-looking forest plant appeared healthier than the ones we had at home.

One of the most abundant groups of understory plants are the heliconias. More than 150 species are found in the New World, the majority of which grow in areas of high sunlight. Thus they are often seen along riverbanks. Their leaves are long and slender, similar in shape to the leaf of a banana tree. Small species stand no taller than 18 inches (46 cm), while large species may reach 18 feet (6 m). When in bloom, they are easy to spot due to their bright red, yellow, and orange inflorescences. They aren't called flowers, because the actual flowers of heliconias are small, pale colored, and often hard to see. The colorful inflorescences are used instead to attract the hummingbirds that pollinate heliconias. They grow on structures called bracts, which surround the flowers. The arrangement of bracts and flowers varies. Some grow straight up, providing a splash of color close to the forest floor. Others dangle from long stems and resemble strings of brightly colored firecrackers. The bracts of upright heliconias often fill with water and form little ponds. It does not take long for aquatic insect larvae to move in to these tiny pools and use them as a temporary habitat.

Many smaller trees populate the shady understory. Some have tall crowns that attempt to fill the gaps between the flat-crowned canopy

Heliconias are typically pollinated by hummingbirds.
Every act in the rain forest, though, carries its risks. Here,
a rufous-tailed hummingbird barely escapes the strike of an
eyelash viper that doesn't want to share its perch.

A Peruvian Indian woman weaves a fan from the leaves of a palm tree. The many types of palms found in the understory provide valuable raw materials, as well as tasty fruits.

species growing above. Some of these trees are mature and have reached their full height. Others are young, still inching their way up to a higher level. Among the most abundant of the full-grown understory trees are the palms. It would be difficult to walk through an Amazonian forest without passing dozens of different palms. In the New World alone, there are more than a thousand species. To the rain forest's human residents they are easily the most valuable group of trees. They provide wood for construction, bark for flooring, leaves for roof thatching, fiber for weaving, darts for blowguns, and fruits for eating. A single native house may be built of more than seven different palm species, not including the *chambira* palm fiber used to weave the hammock.

Understory Animals

In the patchy light of the understory roam some of the Amazon's largest land animals. Do not expect to see them standing out in the open, howev-

The long probing nose of a tapir sniffs about in search of food. Tapirs are large and strong. As the biggest mammals found on the forest floor, they have been the frequent targets of hunters.

er. Hunting by humans has caused most animals to become extremely wary—especially near cities or villages. Large predators, such as the forest cats and boa constrictors and anacondas, add to the pressure.

The largest land mammal is the tapir, known in Spanish as *sacha vaca*, or forest cow. These powerful animals may weigh more than 500 pounds (227 kg). They spend most of their time foraging for leaves and fruits. The understory offers the tapir a wide selection of vegetation within easy reach. Although they give the appearance of being slow moving and docile, they can run quite fast. If frightened, they often plunge into a river or stream to escape. The upper lip of the tapir's mouth is extended into a snout that curves around. It acts like a mini–elephant trunk. Another unique feature of this animal is the high-pitched whistling noise it makes. It is a form of communication and sounds more like a teakettle than a quarter-ton (254-kg) rainforest animal.

Smaller in size are the peccaries, piglike animals that travel in groups along the forest floor. The white-lipped peccary is often found in herds as large as two to three hundred members. Although wary and not aggressive, these 60 to 90 pound (27–41 kg) animals can inflict a painful bite with their large canine teeth. Peccaries spend the daylight hours rooting around the shrubs and undergrowth, searching for fruit, palm nuts, and snails.

Rain forests have their share of rodents. But their shy natures make them hard to see. The paca is a nocturnal, or nighttime, forager that weighs from 10 to 25 pounds (4.5–11.4 kg). It has dark brown fur with rows of white spots. Pacas live in pairs and feed on fallen fruits, nuts, and seeds that they find while roaming among the leaf litter. Their habit of burying nuts for future use makes them important seed dispersers. For example, pacas and agoutis are among the few animals able to gnaw through the thick woody fruit of the Brazil nut tree to reach the seeds or nuts inside. Since these fruits are almost the size and weight of a bowling ball, they do not fall far from the tree. Their seeds are dispersed to new areas only when one of these rodents chews through to a seed, buries it elsewhere, then fails to return to it. Agoutis are smaller and are most often seen at dawn and dusk. They are less wary in low-light settings.

A predator that feeds on all rainforest rodents, as well as an assortment of birds, reptiles, and mammals, is the red-tailed boa. Also known as the boa constrictor, this is a handsome heavy-bodied snake with alternating light and dark bands that run the length of its body. At the tail these bands change from a dark brown to a vivid reddish brown. The dark and light coloring of this snake provides it with the perfect camouflage necessary to

Boa constrictors forage among the branches of understory trees, as well as on the ground. Their slow movements and camouflage patterns make them a predator that is difficult to detect.

escape notice among the leaves and debris. Like all boas, it holds its prey by grabbing it with its mouth and teeth. Then it quickly loops coils of its muscular body around the animal. As the boa continues to squeeze, the captured prey is unable to breathe and quickly gives in. Then it is swallowed whole. The heavier adult snakes are most often found on the ground. The young often forage among the understory branches. The red-tailed boa seldom grows larger than 10 feet (3 m). But it is very strong and can overcome animals even as large as a peccary.

Of all the hunters that stalk their prey throughout the understory, the largest and most feared is the jaguar. Reaching a weight of more than 300 pounds (136 kg), an adult male jaguar can bring down almost any animal in the rain forest. Sadly, it is an animal that has suffered terrible losses due to hunting for its skins. Although it is against the law for people to bring the pelt of a jaguar or any other spotted cat into the United States, I am constantly shocked at the number of tourists who continue to buy them while in the Amazon. This only encourages native hunters to continue trapping and killing them.

While the jaguar is the largest rainforest cat, it is by no means the only one. Pumas, also known as mountain lions, are found throughout the rain forest. But they are very seldom seen. Both the ocelot and the margay are spotted forest cats that grow no larger than 25 to 30 pounds (11.4–13.6 kg). The jaguarundi has dark fur, but with no spots. It is about the size of a large house cat. Opportunistic predators, they feed on whatever they happen to find. These jungle cats will eat a wide variety of prey including snakes, lizards, frogs, turtles, rodents, and mammals. They are limited only by their own size and strength.

Until very recently, studies were restricted to the understory. That is no longer the case, though, as technology now allows researchers to access the canopy. Secrets are just beginning to be revealed about life in the next rainforest layer, the canopy.

Swift and agile, the jaguar is the largest rainforest cat. A solitary predator, it usually preys on deer, tapirs, capybaras, fish, and birds. But it has been known to pursue cattle, horses, and dogs. Thus it has been hunted, almost to extinction, by the rain forest's native residents.

Huge vines called lianas
follow the light and
eventually make their
way up to the canopy.
Sometimes they connect
the crowns of many trees.

Chapter Five

THE CANOPY AND BEYOND

*T*he canopy trees face an entirely different set of challenges than those of the layers below. Their bushy crowns block the glare of the tropical sun. Together, they form a buffer zone. They protect the lower parts of the forest, leaving themselves exposed to a variety of conditions. They must bear the unpredictable weather of the rain forest—shifting temperatures, high humidity, rainfall, and wind—on a daily basis. As a result, species of canopy trees have developed their own adaptations that aid them in survival. Their leaves tend to be smaller and thicker, which keeps them from drying out. This is important where the air is hotter, drier, and moving about more frequently. Also, many of their seeds are light and thus scattered by the wind. The canopy trees often use their great heights to their advantage.

From the air it appears as if the tops of the trees occur at exactly the same place. The trees seem to be all the same height. However, it is actually an irregular ceiling with the crowns occurring at different places. From within the forest one can see this more clearly. The trees and their branches are not crammed together. Neighboring trees have a margin of space separating their crowns. This gap is called tree shyness.

I have been fortunate to spend part of my time in Amazonian forests exploring in the canopy itself. This is made possible by a quarter-mile-long (0.4-km) canopy walkway opened in the early 1990s in northeastern Peru. Managed by Explorama Tours and the Amazon Center for Environmental

Education and Research (ACEER), it offers access to the canopy level 120 feet (36 m) above the forest floor. By crossing the tracks that span the distance from one emergent tree to the next, I gradually made my way up into the treetops. I could then see that the trees formed a wall of protection. But it took the increasing wind of an approaching storm to explain why.

Large trees are no more static than large buildings. Skyscrapers are built to sway in the wind just like big canopy trees. The trees sometimes rock back and forth during tropical windstorms. Their huge crowns are blown in many directions. This could help explain tree shyness. When the wind blows and the moving branches of neighboring trees come in contact, the tips and ends break off. As the canopy tends to be a very windy place, the treetops are constantly rubbing against one another. The result is a gap between neighboring crowns.

Canopy trees are often filled with fruits, which will attract animals from all over the forest. Even when not bearing fruit, these trees are home to thousands of insects that live both in and on them. Fruits and insects form the main diet of many species of birds and monkeys that travel throughout the canopy in search of their next meal. There are more than forty species of monkeys in the Amazon Basin. They range from the tiny pygmy marmoset that barely weighs a quarter of a pound (100 g) to the black spider monkey that approaches 30 pounds (13.5 kg). Along with birds, they are the major seed dispersers of canopy trees. They knock down and drop partially eaten fruits as they forage. Or they eat entire fruits only to excrete the seeds later.

Howler monkeys are a common canopy resident. They feed mostly on leaves and are able to blend in to the crown of a tree. It is often easier to hear this very vocal species than it is to see them. Weighing 15 to 20 pounds (6.8–9 kg), these large monkeys have big heads and an expanded throat. At dawn and dusk both males and females of a troop "chorus" together. This involves sending out a loud roar that carries through the forest and helps to establish their territory. Sometimes a disturbance such

Canopy walkways, such as this one in northeastern Peru, have been constructed at several rainforest sites throughout the world. For the first time, scientists and tourists alike have quick and easy access to the upper layers of the tropical forest.

as a thunderstorm will also trigger their hoots and howls. Howler monkeys are often hunted and killed for their meat. More and more, they are becoming a threatened rainforest species.

Certain groups of New World monkeys display an adaptation especially

Howlers are stout, bearded monkeys with a hunched appearance and thick fur. Their hair, depending on the species, is typically black, brown, or red.

helpful for life in the trees. Their prehensile tail serves as a sort of fifth, or extra, limb. Their tails are able to function almost like a hand. They can curl around objects and grasp onto them. Some of the larger species such as the spider, wooly, and howler monkeys have prehensile tails that are bare on the underside. This makes it even more effective as a gripping tool. Spider monkeys often use their tails to move through the forest, hanging and swinging beneath the branches as they zip along. Howlers more often use their tails as an anchor. It keeps them safe and stable when they are perched high in a tree.

To a certain extent, forest birds have also had to become climbers, in order to forage along twigs and branches. An adaptation that aids them in this task is their specialized toe structure. Birds such as woodpeckers, trogons, toucans, and parrots have two toes that point forward and two that point backward. This makes for a much more balanced grip than the three toes in front and one in back found on most birds. In fact, some parrots may even hang upside down for hours as they forage.

Toucans are often seen in the canopy. Their oversized beaks make them hard to miss. Along with their large-billed relatives, the toucanets and aracaris, there are more than thirty species found in the basin. They survive mostly on fruit, although they will eat the occasional insect. The large bill may seem clumsy at first, but when picking fruits toucans can use them with precision. If small, the fruit is plucked with the tip of the beak and then tossed back into the throat with a flip of the head. If large, the sharp edge of the beak is used to cut off pieces of the fruit that are then inched forward to

Toucans eat the fruits of up to one hundred species of plants and trees. Most of their moisture comes from the fruit and not from drinking water.

Looking up from ground level at a ceiba tree, the epiphyte-covered branches don't even begin for 80 to 90 feet (24.3–27.4 m). The crowns of emergents such as this extend even higher than the canopy layer.

the tip and tossed back. Toucans often forage together in groups of ten to twelve birds. Some, such as the aracaris, even sleep together in hollow trees.

Emergents

The true rainforest giants whose crowns reach higher than the canopy layer are called emergent trees. In the Amazon they may stand 150 feet (45 m) tall. Two emergent species are the Brazil nut tree and the silk cotton, or kapok, tree. Unfortunately, the large straight trunks and the immense girth of silk cotton trees made them prime targets for lumber companies, which took the biggest trees first. Few of these giants remain after the decades of logging in the Amazon Basin. Brazil nut trees have fared better, perhaps because their nuts are harvested and sold.

Naturally, the tops of the emergent trees offer the best vantage point in the entire forest. The crown is also one of the forest's safest and hardest-to-reach places. For these reasons, it is one of the favorite nesting spots of the harpy eagle. At 20 pounds (9 kg) and with a wingspan of nearly 6 feet (1.8 m), this bird can swoop down onto its tree-dwelling prey at speeds exceeding 50 miles per hour (80 km/hr). It snatches the prey from its perch then crushes it in its talons. The favorite prey of harpy eagles are sloths and monkeys. But they also eat other animals such as opossums and porcupines. Unlike other raptors that spot their prey by soaring overhead, the harpy eagle keeps watch from the treetops. It may fly from one perch to another, always on the lookout for its next meal. Once a kill is made using its huge hooked claws, the harpy eagle wields its razor-sharp beak to skin the animal. The meat is then eaten over a period of several days.

High from its canopy perch, a harpy eagle surveys the tangled branches of the forest for prey. It strikes quietly and with fantastic speed, plucking monkeys or sloths before they are aware of the danger.

Drip tips, as seen on this fig leaf, help rainforest plants quickly remove water from their leaves—a simple yet essential adaptation.

Chapter Six

EQUIPPED FOR SURVIVAL

*T*he leaves that make up the forest's foliage have adapted to the heat and wind they face. They are able to retain the moisture that is so essential to their survival. A common adaptation seen on many understory leaves is the drip tip. This is a pointed, narrow spout on the end of the leaf that aids in the removal of water. The upper surfaces of leaves are also smooth to speed the runoff. If the leaf stays constantly wet, it is much easier for small plants such as mosses and lichens to gain a foothold. When these plants grow on leaves they block the sunlight and decrease the rate of photosynthesis. The drip tip helps keep the leaves clean and dry. This is especially important to species that live in the damp and humid understory.

All trees must replace fallen, dead, or eaten leaves. To avoid being constantly eaten by insects and canopy browsers that prefer young leaves, most Amazonian trees produce their new growth all at once in what is called a flush. The period between flushes may be many months or even more than a year. New leaves are often softer and red in color. By not offering tender new leaf growth throughout the year, trees force leaf eaters to search in other areas. When the new growth of foliage bursts out all at once, the tree stands a better chance of being overlooked amidst all the other trees. If it is discovered, not all of its leaves will be eaten. Plus the flush may be discovered too late, after the new leaves have grown older and stiffer. The same strategy is often observed in flowering and fruiting.

Tropical foliage is the target of predators of all sizes.
Here, leaf miners have dug a series of trails through a leaf.

Individual members of the same species are often widely scattered. This decreases competition, or the use of the same resources by both the parent tree and its offspring. However, in order to create offspring, the flower of one tree must be fertilized by the pollen of another tree of the same species. This is called cross-pollination. The bees, bats, and butterflies that assist in this process have to be able to find the flowers. This is made easier if the distant trees flower and then bear fruit at the same time. The same advantages seen in leaves produced in flushes apply to fruit appearing all at once. Because so many are available at one time, some are sure to escape notice and aid in creating the next generation.

Trees send out their seeds in many different ways. Aerial dispersal, or scattering the seeds to the wind, is especially suited to the trees of the canopy. Not all canopy trees use this method. But those that do have evolved seeds that are lightweight and aerodynamic. Some are wide and flat and act like a single wing. They dip toward the ground in a wide curving sweep. Others have two or more flattened prongs that cause them to spin slowly on the way down like a tiny helicopter. The silk cotton tree releases seeds inside light, fluffy strands of material. This gauzy cushion floats down on the air currents and is carried away from the fruit and the tree that bore it.

Hanging Gardens

In the rain forest, there is only so much room. So some plants, called epiphytes, have adapted in a unique way. They grow directly on other plants and trees. They come in many shapes and sizes and include bromeliads, aroids, orchids, cactuses, mosses, ferns, lichen, and liverworts. Lacking soil from which to grow, epiphytes cling to their hosts with special roots that

A wide variety of creatures help to pollinate the trees and plants of the rain forest. Here a large orchid bee has been drawn to a blossom.

Tank bromeliads are common in the canopy, where they trap water in the center of their leaves. Like other epiphytes, they do not harm their host tree. They only use part of its surface on which to grow.

Attracted by the flowers of this epiphyte, a coppery-headed emerald hummingbird greedily sucks up the nectar. In the process of feeding, pollen rubs off on the bird, which it then carries to the next plant or flower.

provide a firm hold. The essential nutrients they need are taken directly from the humid, moisture-laden air. In some cases, epiphytes form their own soil over time by gathering debris and airborne particles at their bases.

Bromeliads are plants in the pineapple family. Their leaves typically grow the way a pineapple's does, in a spiral around a central base. Some members of this group are called tank bromeliads because water becomes trapped where their wide leaves meet and form a sort of basin in the center. In especially large bromeliads, these tanks may hold gallons of rainwater. However, the tightly overlapping leaf bases don't trap only water. They hold fallen leaves, pieces of twigs, dead insects, fragments of bark, and whatever else happens to fall in. Nutrients from the breakdown of these materials help feed the bromeliad. But not all of the matter stays within the tank. Some of this organic debris becomes trapped under the plant and the branch of the host tree. As the material decays, mosses and other small plants take root in it. They provide a wider area where even more falling material can cling and eventually break down. After years or decades, there may be several inches of soil on the branch. This nutrient-rich soil is such a valuable resource that many trees tap into it. They send roots directly from their branches. These roots burrow into the dirt and remove whatever nutrients they can.

The tops of canopy branches are sometimes covered with bromeliads and other epiphytes. At the cloud forest of Rancho Grande in Venezuela, I have seen tree branches where every available inch of space was covered in epiphytes. Cloud forests occur at elevations of several thousand feet and higher. There, the trees are continually shrouded with mist—ideal growing conditions for epiphytes. When in flower, some epiphytes produce large showy red blooms to attract their hummingbird pollinators. Many orchids, however, rely on beautiful metallic blue-green bees. No matter who carries the pollen, both parties benefit. It is another example of mutualism in the rain forest. The pollinator gets a meal, and the epiphyte is able to reproduce.

Change occurs within the rain forest on both a large and a small scale. Animals such as these leafcutter ants alter the forest only slightly, marching along a branch with their prized sections of leaves.

Chapter Seven

AN EVER-CHANGING WORLD

T he rain forest of the Amazon Basin is the largest remaining tropical forest in the world. Some of its tallest trees have endured for centuries. These old specimens can give the impression that they are here to stay. You might assume that, beyond the slow process of growth, the rain forest is a stable, consistent place where very little alters. In truth, the rain forest is a dynamic world, meaning it is always changing. Some changes are immediate, while others can occur over hundreds of years. Some help the forest and maintain its health, while others create long-term damage.

There are many events that can affect the growth of both large tracts of forest and very small patches. Harmful changes may be the result of natural causes. Earthquakes are not an uncommon event in the Amazon Basin. Landslides and mudslides cause less damage, but take place more frequently. They sometimes make driving a mountain road quite dangerous. While driving along the eastern slopes of the Andes in Ecuador and Peru, I have seen long scars in the hillsides. These slashes of exposed red earth are set off by the green forest growing on all sides.

Powerful winds are another destructive force. They sometimes strike Amazonian forests with the strength of a cyclone. Rainforest giants are toppled. Treetops are snapped off. Huge limbs are torn from their trunks.

Slash and burn agriculture is a short-term solution with long-term effects. The forest may take decades to recover. But many rainforest residents feel they are offered few other options.

Immense vines known as lianas, some as thick as trees from decades of growth, often connect the crowns of several canopy trees and cause them all to fall at once. In a matter of hours a storm can change the face of a large portion of forest. Such storms are not a constant threat, as they do not occur frequently by our standards. Twenty to fifty years may pass between the wild windstorms. To most people this is a long time. However, to a forest that has endured for thousands of years and that has trees more than two hundred years old, recovery can take decades.

The changes created by humans are more frequent and easier to see. A boat trip along the Amazon or any of its tributaries will quickly show the impact of people. Small farming homesteads, or *chacras*, dot the riverbanks. Forest is cleared to provide land for growing bananas, plantains, manioc, papaya, corn, beans, and other crops. On a larger scale, sizable pieces of forest have been cleared for cattle. Once the trees are cut down, the area is burned to release the nutrients locked in the trunks and branches back into the soil. Then the land can be used for several seasons as a pasture. However, it quickly becomes unusable due to the leaching, or draining away, of necessary nutrients. Large-scale lumbering operations have similar effects. They open areas of the forest to direct sunlight. In other forms of timber harvesting, individual trees or species may be the target. Rough roads are built to access them and bring in heavy equipment. After the harvest, settlers sometimes follow these roads and establish homesteads. They often cut down more of the forest in their search for raw materials.

The removal of even a single tree changes the forest. Sunlight is able to strike parts of the ground once shaded by branches and bushy leaves. Light fuels the forest. It spurs growth and drives photosynthesis. It even affects what species will grow where.

Light Gaps

From the inside, the rain forest appears to be bathed in a constant twilight. Here and there a stray sunbeam will reach the understory. But generally, the place is very dim. Occasionally, though, large openings are created in the forest by either people or the forces of nature. If a canopy tree grows old and dies, it will eventually fall to the ground. The same may occur with a tree of any size or to a large limb that has become diseased. After the loud crack and crash have faded and the leaves and debris settle, the change becomes clear. Light starts streaming in. It is now available to a new part of the forest. Its sudden appearance sets off a chain of events. Over the course of the following days and weeks, the entire character of that small part of the forest will be altered.

In the rain forest, the ground contains many seeds that have built up over the years. Some are brought by the wind. Others are left there by rodents, much as squirrels bury acorns in temperate regions. Still others are dropped by monkeys, birds, or any of the animals that feed in the branches above. Studies have shown that about 10 square feet (1 sq m) of rain forest may hold more than a thousand seeds. When light suddenly reaches the forest floor, many of those seeds germinate and burst into life.

Not all of the seeds are living though, especially after years of being buried and exposed to predators. Seeds from canopy species tend to live only for a few weeks. If they do not germinate during this brief period, they have lost their chance. Thus, they must either land in a gap or one needs to be created around them soon after they fall. However, a whole group of plants is specially adapted to the rare or random opening of tree gaps. These are called secondary forest species. Examples are heliconia, mimosa, cecropia, and the kapok tree. The seeds of these species remain alive for years. Their seedlings sprout quickly and fill the gap.

In addition to this "seed bank" stored in the soil, the tree fall gap is also colonized by new seeds, by shoots growing from stumps and branches, and by those pre-existing seedlings that weren't damaged when the tree fell to the forest floor. With this combined response, the ground exposed in a gap may be covered with lush growth in only a few weeks. In a few years, those same seedlings will be trees 30 to 40 feet (9–12 m) high. Nothing happens in isolation. When a tree falls, it is just the beginning of a series of changes that patch of forest will undergo.

Succession

The opening of a light gap, and the burst of growth that follows, is just one of the forest's many changes. The tangled mat of greenery that fills the gap is just a temporary stage. Over time that patch of forest will play host to a series of different species. Quick-growing sprouts soon develop into woody saplings and small trees. Big enough eventually to create shade of their own, they decrease the light available to seeds and younger plants. The lower light level restricts new growth mostly to those species that are shade tolerant. These include many types of palms, various gingers, some heliconia, breadfruit trees, and also cacao or the chocolate tree. Thus the makeup and appearance of the gap change once again. The process of growth and

With the opening of a tree fall gap, light, once barred by the thick crowns, comes streaming onto the forest floor. The trunk of the fallen tree may soon be covered with shrubs and vines.

species replacement continues until the gap is occupied by mature forest. This continual evolution of the forest is known as succession.

In the cycle of change a forest experiences, scientists have identified certain stages of succession. One is the primary forest, which refers to the forest in its original state. Undisturbed or virgin forest means the same thing. When an area is colonized by new species, its forest is then called secondary. Such forests tend to have fewer tree species and thicker undergrowth.

But this presumes the change follows a standard or regular pattern. But rain forests are far too complex and unpredictable. They are affected by soil, rainfall, wind, elevation, drainage, and even the element of chance, to name just a few of the factors. In general, the mature tropical forest is marked by high diversity, tall trees, and less dense vegetation on the ground. However, the constant opening and reforestation of gaps makes most tropical forests a patchwork of primary and secondary forests. Different parts of the forest face different types of change.

The rain forest is a world made up of millions of parts. Plants, trees, animals, and insects are just some of its building blocks. They all depend on one another for survival. They alter the forest or must react and adapt to its constant cycles of change. There is still much to be learned about how all of these parts fit together. Only with a complete understanding of its many pieces can we protect, preserve, and ensure the rain forest's future.

All of an ecosystem's life-forms are connected, drawn together in a delicate balance. This tarantula and the katydid it has just captured are part of a vast web of life that must be honored and preserved.

GLOSSARY

abiotic: nonliving; abiotic elements include rainfall, temperature, and humidity.

aerodynamic: specially designed to fly or glide through the air.

aroid: a plant in the philodendron family.

biomass: the weight of all the living things that make up a population or that live in a particular habitat.

bract: colorful structures on plants that are used to attract pollinators but are not flowers.

bromeliad: a plant in the pineapple family that often has straplike leaves that grow in a spiral.

canopy: all the crowns of the tall mature trees that are above the understory and form the "roof" of the rain forest.

carrion: rotting meat, such as the remains of dead animals.

cauliflory: flowering and fruiting directly from a tree trunk.

chacra: a small plot of land that is farmed along a riverbank.

climax forest: the type of woodland that occurs at the end of succession.

cross-pollination: the process through which the flower of one plant or tree is fertilized with the pollen of another.

decomposer: an organism that breaks down dead tissue into its basic components or elements.

decomposition: the process of breaking down dead tissues.

drip tip: an elongated point or extension at the end of a leaf that helps it to shed water.

ecosystem: all the living organisms as well as the nonliving parts of their environment within a given area or community.

emergent: a tall rainforest tree whose crown sticks up and above the rest of the canopy.

epiphyte: a plant that grows on a tree or other plant, using it only for support.

forest floor: the ground, topsoil, and leaf litter of the forest.

fungi: organisms whose bodies are hyphal strands and whose reproductive structures are called mushrooms.

germinate: sprout, as in a seed.

hypha: the threadlike body of a fungus.

inflorescence: a cluster of flowers and their associated structures.

invertebrate: an animal without a backbone.

leaf litter: the buildup of leaves and leaf debris on top of the forest topsoil.

liana: a large, woody forest vine.

lichen: an organism that is part green alga and part fungus living together mutualistically.

light gap: an opening in the forest that allows more light to reach the forest floor.

macroinvertebrate: an organism without a backbone that is relatively large such as an insect or spider.

mutualism: a relationship in which two different species live in close association with one another so that both benefit.

mycelium: a network of many strands of fungal hyphae.

mycorrhizae: a group of fungi that form a mutualistic relationship with tree roots, providing them with soil nutrients in return for plant sugars.

nitrogen-fixing bacteria: bacteria that have a mutualistic relationship with the roots of legumes, providing them with nitrogen in return for plant sugars.

opportunistic: feeding on whatever is available.

organic: living.

photosynthesis: the process by which green plants, when exposed to the sun, use chlorophyll to convert water and carbon dioxide from the atmosphere into sugars and oxygen.

pollination: the transfer of pollen leading to fertilization.

primary forest: forest that has not been cut or disturbed. Also known as undisturbed or virgin forest.

protozoan: a one-celled, microscopic organism.

rain shadow effect: process through which clouds release their moisture while trying to pass over mountains with the result that one side of the mountains is very wet and the other extremely dry.

saprophyte: a decomposer or organism that breaks down dead tissue for its nutrients.

secondary forest: woodland that after time replaces primary forest in the process of succession.

shade tolerance: the ability of plants or trees to grow successfully in low-light situations.

spore: a structure released by a fungus or moss that functions like a seed to start a new organism.

succession: process through which a forest or patch of forest changes over the course of many years.

tank bromeliad: an epiphyte whose leaves are arranged so that water is trapped in the center of the plant.

tree shyness: the gap found between the crowns of canopy trees due to branches breaking off from constant contact with neighboring branches.

tree fall gap: an opening caused by the collapse or felling of a tree that allows light to stream down onto the forest floor.

understory: layer of the rain forest that features small to medium-sized trees that are taller than the shrubs and shorter than the canopy trees.

SPECIES AT A GLANCE

Agouti (*Dasyprocta* spp.): A group of several species of forest floor rodents that look like large tailless squirrels and that feed on fruits, seeds, and nuts.

Anaconda (*Eunectes murinus*): The largest and heaviest snake in the world with recorded lengths of up to 28 feet (8.5 m). Known as the water boa due to its fondness for swampy and aquatic habitats.

Coatimundi (*Nasua nasua*): A member of the raccoon family reaching 15 pounds (6.8 kg) and with a long, narrow snout and very long upright tail. Coatis feed on almost everything and forage both on the ground and in the trees.

Harpy eagle (*Harpia harpyja*): The world's largest eagle, which nests in emergent trees and feeds on sloths, monkeys, and other arboreal rainforest animals.

Jaguar (*Panthera onca*): The largest spotted cat and terrestrial predator of the rain forest at 300 pounds (136 kg). It hunts large mammals and a variety of other prey both during the day and at night.

Jaguarundi (*Felis yagouarundi*): A predatory cat that varies from brown to gray to red in color and that weighs up to 20 pounds (9 kg). It feeds mostly on small mammals, birds, and reptiles.

Ocelot (*Felis pardalis*): A forest cat with a spotted and striped pelt that ranges in size from 20 to 30 pounds (9–13.6 kg). It hunts mainly at night on the ground feeding primarily on small mammals.

Oropendola (*Psarocolius* spp.): A group of several species of brightly colored birds with alternating dark and bright yellow plumage. They are known for their long hanging woven nests that are made close to one another.

Paca (*Agouti paca*): A large spotted rodent of the forest floor with a heavy piglike body reaching 10 to 25 pounds (4.5–11.3 kg). Pacas are widely hunted for their tasty meat.

Peccary (*Tayassu* spp.): Large piglike animal that ranges from 40 to 90 pounds (18.1–40.8 kg) and feeds on both animal and plant matter. There is both a collared peccary (*T. tajacu*) and a white-lipped peccary (*T. pecari*) in the Amazon Basin.

Puma (*Felis concolor*): Also known as the mountain lion, this is the same large tawny cat that is found in the western Untied States. Weighing up to 250 pounds (113.4 kg), it feeds primarily on large mammals.

Red-tailed boa (*Boa constrictor*): A common nonvenomous snake with dark and light brown bands that grows up to 10 feet (3 m) long. It feeds on mammals, birds, and lizards, which it kills by squeezing them to death.

Tapir (*Tapirus terrestris*): The largest terrestrial rainforest mammal, weighing 500 pounds (226.8 kg) or more. The tapir has an elongated upper lip that can grab and aid in feeding. It is related to the rhinoceros and feeds on fruits and plants and browses leaves.

FIND OUT MORE

BOOKS

Albert, Toni. *The Remarkable Rainforest: An Active-Learning Book for Kids*. Mechanicsburg, PA: Trickle Creek, 1994.

Aldis, Rodney. *Rainforests*. Parsippany, NJ: Silver Burdett, 1991.

Ayensu, Edward S., ed. *Jungles*. New York: Crown Publishers, 1980.

Forsyth, Adrian, and Ken Miyata. *Tropical Nature*. New York: Simon & Schuster, 1984.

Goodman, Susan E., and Michael J. Doolittle. *Bats, Bugs, and Biodiversity*. New York: Anthenum Books for Young Readers, 1995.

Landau, Elaine. *Tropical Forest Mammals*. New York: Childrens Press, 1996.

Landsman, Susan. *Survival! In the Jungle*. New York: Avon, 1993.

Lasky, Kathryn. *The Most Beautiful Roof in the World*. San Diego: Gulliver Green, 1997.

Mitchell, Andrew W. *The Enchanted Canopy*. New York: Macmillan Publishing Co., 1986.

Newman, Arnold. *Tropical Rainforest*. New York: Facts On File, 1990.

Perry, Donald. *Life above the Jungle Floor*. New York: Simon & Schuster, Inc., 1986.

WEBSITES

abcteach
http://abcteach.com/index.html

Animals of the Rainforest
www.animalsoftherainforest.org

Exploring the Vast Amazon
http://tqjunior.thinkquest.org/5128

A Journey through the Rainforest
www.photo.net/cr/rara

Rainforests
www.edu.pe.ca/fortune/rain.htm

Rainforest Explorer
http://rainforestexplorer.com/RF/RF1.html

Toucan.org
www.toucan.org

ORGANIZATIONS

Conservation International
1919 M Street, NW
Suite 600
Washington, D.C. 20036
(202) 912-1000
www.conservation.org

Friends of the Earth
1025 Vermont Avenue, NW
Washington, D.C. 20005
(877) 843-8687
www.for.org

The Nature Conservancy
International Conservation Program
4245 North Fairfax Drive
Arlington, VA 22203-1606
(703) 841-5300
www.tnc.org

Missouri Botanical Garden
P.O. Box 299
St. Louis, MO 63166
(314) 577-5100
www.mobot.org

Rainforest Alliance
65 Bleecker Street
New York, NY 10012
(212) 677-1900
www.rainforest-alliance.org

Sierra Club
85 Second Street, 2nd Floor
San Francisco, CA 94105-3441
(415)977-5500
www.sierraclub.com

ABOUT THE AUTHOR

Dr. James L. Castner is a tropical biologist-writer-photographer and adjunct professor of biology at Pittsburg State University. He has traveled throughout the rain forests of South and Central America, but has focused primarily on the Amazon Basin of Peru. His main interest is how insects defend themselves, especially with the use of camouflage and mimicry. His unique photos of rainforest insects have appeared in *National Geographic*, *Natural History*, *International Wildlife*, *Ranger Rick*, and *Kids Discover* magazines.

Dr. Castner has spent the past several years writing books about insects and the rain forest. He often conducts educational workshops and leads students and teachers on visits to the Tropics. As part of his desire to work with younger students, he is completing his secondary certification in science and Spanish. He plans to finish his career teaching a combination of middle school, high school, and college students.

INDEX